Reflections........In A Sea Of Words

My Diary 2.Wish of a dying man 3. A Romantic Microwave 4. Did you smile today 5. When the music stops 6. WHY! OH WHY! DO I LOVE YOU............ 7.The Pianist 8. Floating on the sails of eternity 9.Right and left I walked 10.Global warming 11. There is a hole in the sky.... 12.The Sandstorm 13. The Arches and gate 14.My blues have just begun 15. No Airlines ever come here 16. The gift of dream 17. The soup was too spicy 18. Can I have a drink tonight 19. There are beautiful girls 20.Dream.......to wake me up 21.Handicrafts.......of Love

Mukul

Made with ❤ on the BookLeaf Publishing Platform
www.bookleafpub.in
www.bookleafpub.com

Dedication

This work is dedicated to someone who made me realize the difference between loving someone and being loved. The one who inundated me with unconditional love, I dedicate this work to my wife- "Veena".

Veena, you are the epitome of what it means to love and to be loved. Through the course of our journey together, you have shown me the profound beauty of unconditional love. Your unwavering support, selflessness, and boundless affection have been the cornerstones upon which our relationship stands strong. From the moment I met you, it was clear that you were a beacon of light in my life. Your kindness and compassion have been a constant source of inspiration, guiding me through the ups and downs of life with grace and poise. Your ability to love unconditionally has taught me that true love does not seek reciprocation but finds joy in the act of giving itself freely.

In every smile, every gentle touch, and every word of encouragement, you have embodied the essence of love. Your love is not just a feeling; it is a powerful force that transforms, heals, and uplifts. It is your love that has given me the strength to overcome challenges and the courage to pursue my dreams.

You have shown me that love is not measured by grand

gestures but by the little things - the quiet moments we share, the laughter that fills our home, and the silent understanding that binds us together. It is in these everyday moments that I have come to understand the true depth of your love.

As I dedicate this work to you, I am reminded of the countless ways you have enriched my life. Your love has been a beacon of hope, a source of comfort, and a testament to the power of human connection. It is because of you that I have come to appreciate the beauty of being loved and the joy of loving in return

Preface

This anthology was created when the world was being
 created....
When the humans felt a sublime emotion
Emotion of love...
It has been flowing since times unknown
In the heart
Like a Sea, with its tumultuous waves hitting the beach
and it hit me like a wave
and in my silences
I have often reflected
in a Sea of words
Words....that have often touched my heart
as only Poetry can....

This is a collection of poems written in different periods
of my life, mostly when I had to move out due to
requirements of Army service.

Acknowledgements

Gratitude to love. the emotion that triggers a surge of emotions- Happiness and joy

Gratitude and Thanks to one who supported me all my life, and yet, I couldn't thank her enough

Gratitude and thanks to all those who have shared my Journey so far...My friends & children

Gratitude to publishers, who made this book possible..

Gratitude to readers, who are setting out to experience something special, and would help me improve with their feedback and comments

A special thanks to my service in Indian Army, which made sure I remain separated for long times, and rekindling the romance

I would like to acknowledge support of Ideogram to help generate AI generated cover.

Thanks

1. MY DIARY

MY DIARY

This is a Diary
but this does not record
events,
appointments, or even achievements

This is a string
with beads of thoughts and emotions
my little joys, trepidations of my heart
and records
words , that tell you
what I want to say
words that fail to tell you
what I want to say
as also words, which mean
much more than what they
could ever say

When I write
the pen moves to the rhythm
of my heart beat
the ink that flows out
reflects
the gush of emotions

leaving me as quiet
as Sea

After its waves rise high
and crash on the Beach

I
may be in any part of the world
TO YOU
Through my words
I try to reach......

2. WISH OF A DYING MAN

WISH OF A DYING MAN...........
When I die....
do not close my eyes
because
even in my death
I can not bear it
that I may not see you anymore......

When I die......
consign me to the flames
before it is too late
before my arms get stiff
because as I die
I still would yearn
to hold you in my arms......

When I die....
lay me to rest
in your heart
because
I want to live forever
as my muffling heartbeats
synchronise
my love for you

with your beating heart....

The love shall stay forever
because
it is eternal
ethereal
just as you are
when you love me
though
I may be away
Though
I might have gone.......
.

I shall live with you
forever ,in your world
in my words...
and you shall never
ever feel alone

When I die....
do not cry
for that would cause me
pain
and tear me apart
in much the same way
as my Poetry
dying out in your heart

When I die.....
let me
live in your heart
because
love shall live on
for ever and ever

When I die.....
I will not die
because
living in your
loving heart for ever
I shall prove
that

DEATH IS NOT
THE TRUTH, MADE OUT TO BE
BUT
A SWEET LIE......! !

When I die...
close your eyes
and think of me
and my words......
which would be left as incomplete
as me

without you.........as incomplete as this poem

3. A ROMANTIC MICROWAVE

A ROMANTIC MICROWAVE
This microwave oven
is made to love
and romance
as timing it for few minutes
required to bake a cake
switching it on
I can sit
holding your face
in my hands
looking into your eyes
lighting up candles of love
in your eyes

The candles
that I intend to place
on the cake
for you to blow
and another candle
for the ambience
as I swirl you around, to the music
and hold you in my arms.......

frozen in time
letting the seconds chime
till the microwave
lets out the beep
. . . .
you put your fingers
on my lips
for silence
tell the microwave, not to disturb
our dreamy state ,and till eternity
let us sleep

The microwave understands,
and in a few seconds
muffles the beep
IT SURE IS A ROMANTIC MICROWAVE

4.

4. METHOD IN MADNESS......

METHOD IN MADNESS.......
I am in a desert
looking miles ahead
seeing not a soul in sight
not even a tree...

Not even a blade of grass
endless
stretch of Sand Dunes
No tracks
which one could see.........

But only
footsteps, coming to me
from miles yonder
from distant lands

The footsteps
that stop
two feet short of me
I can feel your soft hands
holding mine

taking me along with you

My friends tell me
that loneliness
is playing on my nerves
has
driven me INSANE

But
if my INSANITY, brings you
closer to me
in my thoughts
why, should I
even try to remain
SANE ! !

Because
I am crazy about you
madly in love with you
and in my madness
I have found a way
of being with you.....

5. WHY! OH WHY! DO I LOVE YOU.............

WHY! OH WHY! DO I LOVE YOU................
I love you
  not because I have to
  but because
  I need to love you
  and I want you to know
  this
  because I find that
  the world is cluttered
  with words and thoughts
  flying around aimlessly

But
  I want you to know
  that my world revolves
  around you
  that my words are all
  that I can send to you
  from this place away from you

And maybe
 you will feel my need...........

I need to love you
 because you are all I have
 to get the complete sense of love
 to get me be a complete man

And so I love you
 and I want you to know
 even if
 it is the last thing, you may hear from me.....

I love you so ....

6. DID YOU SMILE TODAY ?

DID YOU SMILE TODAY ?

Did you smile today ?
I guess you must have

I heard a rustle of silk
I felt someone touch my arm
I thought I would kindle a bonfire
The thought made me feel warm

I looked out of window
Waved out to a star
it winked back at me saying
I am with you
Do not think I am too far

I wonder
Why should I get such crazy thoughts
Thought over for a while
I felt someone tap my shoulder

Said, do not get worked up
it is all in my smile

 If you cherish it
in your soul, you must keep
Good Night !
and now let me sleep

7. SO, YOU WOULD NOT SAY.................

SO, YOU WOULD NOT SAY....................
 So
You would not say the words
I yearn to hear from you
Not today...
Maybe never..

But
Can you pause your lips
Can you cover your eyes
that shine
The moment they see me
come round the bend...

Maybe you will tie your hands
But the lashes
Shall invite me
By their movements
Up and down...
Down and up......

What shall you do with your smile
That lights up the sun
On a depressing rainy day
As you look at me ......
And
Set the sun on a euphoric trip
Across the sky

Just like the trip
Of life
We set out together on

Some where on the waves of sea
Are the words, lolling up and down
With the waves and tide
The words that I wish to hear from you

Today and forever..
Till the time
I can overcome my shyness
And
Speak them out
To you

May be not today.....Maybe never...

But
In my smile
You would read
Not only the words
But also the meanings

What it means to be with you....................

8. POEMS FLOAT IN THE CLOUDS

POEMS FLOAT IN THE CLOUDS

And poems do float in the clouds
of the emotions
sometimes silent
sometimes loud ...
and when you hear them in the quiet
of solitude ...
or storm in the sea

all that remains
is a song
that touches your soul
and rewinds to play
the songs you hummed few days ago.....

before
I had to move away......

9. MIRAGE.......

MIRAGE.......

Sometimes
As I think of you
I float through clouds
Sail through light

Walk across the deserts
Of loneliness
With my parched lips
Calling out your name..........

Trying to touch you
My arms falling flail
not able to reach you

I fall on my knees
Looking at you
as I follow a mirage
A vision of yours
And my lips silently whisper your name
Before I am engulfed in
The sea of unconsciousness

A sleep
And I dream of you......

Sometimes....
as I think of you

10. WHEN THE MUSIC STOPS.................................

WHEN THE MUSIC STOPS..............................

When the music stops
The lyrics still linger on..

The words you left behind
For me
Will echo in the songs of spring
That the flowers in full bloom
Shall forever sing.....
Before they wither and fall away.....

The fragrance
Still lingers on
Like a fountain of joy
That springs out
With your thoughts

Leaving me numb, and alone
And your memories
Even as I move out
one more time

But
Am I really gone.. ?
or
still with you
in the twilight zone

I am not so sure!

11. THE PIANIST............

THE PIANIST............
I have a friend whose daughter plays Piano .
When I hear her play the piano ,
 she would tell me .. "Uncle, I am playing this particular
symphony "
and I try to follow the notes.
As she plays
she leads me into a trance

where I do not hear the notes anymore.......
All I can feel
is that I am being transported
on notes of lilting music
to a plane where everything
blends into a harmony...

Yes.......
I am moved into the world
of your thoughts , your love,
where happiness and joy
play on like notes of music
played by her...

And then she would stop.

And there are no notes of piano
that she is playing ...
but your thoughts ,
your memories
play on their own frequency ,
and I can hear the notes of Piano
even
when she is not playing anymore ...
I can see candle lights flicker
where she is sitting smiling
and I feel my hands clapping
in rhythm of gratitude
and thanks to her
for bringing you so close to me ....
My heart tells me she is a great pianist...

12. FLOATING ON THE SAILS OF ETERNITY....................

FLOATING ON THE SAILS OF ETERNITY....................

It has been a long time
since angels spoke to me
it has been a long time
since fairies danced with me

It has been a long time
since someone looked into
my eyes
and found her own images
as reflections in my
dreams

It has been a long time
since someone shook me out
of my dreams of her
to see her in person

It has been a long time
someone read

the words
I wrote for her
and that's how these words
reach you

so

be an angel, spread the sunshine
and let the fairies
dance around me

It has been a long time
since I held you close
for seemingly endless time
as we floated on the
sails of eternity

13. RIGHT AND LEFT I WALKED

RIGHT AND LEFT I WALKED

 Right and left I walked
I walked day and night
Looking at things I could see
marvelling at things out of sight
life is good I thought for a while
when in scorching sun I walked a mile

into every sunshine I could
see some rain
behind every smile
I could feel little pain
right and left I walked
I walked day and night

tired and fatigued
I held your hand
as I crashed out
on the burning sand

you smiled and held me tight
I knew it was for you

that I walked right and left
I walked day and night

14. SHORTEST LOVE LETTER

SHORTEST LOVE LETTER

Whenever I am away
from you
My life is ....

So Blank

Without You

15. ON THE BROOKLYN BRIDGE

ON THE BROOKLYN BRIDGE

Standing
on the Brooklyn bridge
looking at the sky
bejewelled by a necklace of stars
seeing your smile
illuminate the night..........
On the Brooklyn Bridge
where I have never been
where I may never be
but my thoughts
my feelings for you
would travel all over the world
(whenever I am away from you
wherever I may be)
and hold you in my arms....
as your smile holds me enchanted......
whether I am on Eiffel Tower
or The Brooklyn Bridge...........

16. THE SKY IS TOO SMALL

THE SKY IS TOO SMALL.........................
Because
The day I was riding the chariot of Sun, with you by my
side,

the seven horses pulling the chariot were ecstatic driving
us along the sky
 and still there was no end of sky in sight....

And
Then we jumped off the chariot on to the cloud nine ,
and walked hand in hand , we felt the clouds to be too
soft ...too fluffy, and warm...
There were golden swings, hanging down from the
rainbows, and as we sat on them ,

holding on to chains entwined by vibrant flowers, we
could feel the fairies giggling and gushing all over, as
they gently rocked the swing...rocking it to and fro......

Swinging us from one end of the sky to another
And all that happened within a fraction of second that
your eyes looked into mine first time ,

and told me you loved me so

And you would agree with me that if the sky was really
as big as it is made out to be ,
it wouldn't have been possible in a fraction of second.....!

17. I AM NOT FAR AWAY.....................

I AM NOT FAR AWAY.....................

If you look into the mirror
and find
the hue of blush on your cheeks
a feeling of warmth through your skin......
If you do not feel any breeze
and find your "Dupatta"
flowing around your face...
If
you find the 'Bindi'
you stuck on the mirror
stuck on
between your arching brows
and the powder of 'Sindoor'
touching your hairs as
you part them
If
you find
the 'bangles' in your hands
touch you
in some strange way
If you listen to the old melodies

of love
of yearnings, of missing you
on the cassette
I left for you
and if you find your soul being
stirred in some familiar way......
........Do not turn around to see me

in next few moments
you will feel
my hands on your shoulders
wheeling you around...
and telling you
You may be missing me
But I am not far away..........

18. GLOBAL WARMING.........

GLOBAL WARMING..........
It was the coldest day of the year
even
the Sun was shivering
every few seconds
it would go under the blanket of clouds
and jab it like
a stab
the cloud winced in pain
let out a few tears drop
which rolled over the sky
and
froze on the windscreen of my car

The light scattered out,
as if it was a prism
and I could see a rainbow
through my windscreen
and I thought
I saw you smiling at
the other end of the rainbow......

The warmth of the smile

radiated all around , even
The Sun started sweating
and ran across the sky
to dip into the Sea......

The Scientists
all over the world
went into a frenzy
about GLOBAL WARMING.......

And
to think of it
I WAS ONLY THINKING OF YOU................

20. THE JOY OF KEEPING AWAKE.............

THE JOY OF KEEPING AWAKE.............

It is four in the morning
I am yet to sleep
not because I cannot
not because I have to keep awake
but
because my eyes are open
and I can see
you standing by the lake

My mind
tells me, it is not real
you are miles away
my mind also tells me
If I close my eyes
I might find you
in my dreams
coming to stay.....

but I cannot take a chance
what if it does not happen
this way.......

I must keep awake any way......

I must keep awake
looking at you
till you come in person
and make it my day

my mind is angry
and has gone to sleep
my heart smiles within
and lets the joy sink deep........

21. Dream.............to wake me up

Dream............to wake me up

I got up in the morning
to find a smile
on my pillow
smiling at me..
as you sometimes do
before bursting into laughter
at some clumsy thing,
in a clumsy way I do....

As I opened the windows
I was touched
by a touch
that I thought was a ray of Sun
but which touched me like you do ..

it might have been a ray of Sun
that touched me..
but the warmth was yours !

I felt a pinch
on my skin
as I sometimes do
when I want to confirm
whether I am awake or
dreaming
or
awake and dreaming !

but I do not remember
pinching myself
could someone, please tell me
whether I am awake or dreaming
awake and dreaming, or
dreaming that I am awake and dreaming
or, is it simply a dream to wake me up

22. HANDICRAFTS OF LOVE...............

HANDICRAFTS OF LOVE...............

I am impressed
  with a piece of handicraft
  I bought
  just now.....
  The embroidery is superb
  the threads are of gold
  the drawing is a sweet
  romantic story
  in golden threads retold

  something
  like your love for me
  exquisite, beautiful
  adding bounties of love
  and colour
  like embroidery
  with a golden thread

on the fabric of my life

of course, I am aware
that in the process
the needle has often caused you
pain
the threads have often got entangled
in vain....
your eyes have turned misty
as the clouds overhead
burst out in torrential rain

I wish to hold
your hand
and touch my heart
so that I may merge
your pain into my remorse
and let the floodgates
of happiness open, and be it their destiny
to chart out our future course...

23. THE GOLDEN SAND ……….. ………..

THE GOLDEN SAND

………. ……….

The sand here looks
golden

as the morning Sun
emerges out
from behind the hills

Each ray
finds reflection in
each grain of sand
something like your smile
like your touch
as I hold your hand

I can find a wave

of joy
sweeping through every molecule
of my very being
making every moment
of my existence
golden

As you open your eyes
from under the lashes
look at me, as if to tell me

you love me so.......................

24. Reflections.....

Reflections.....

People
have often fantasized over moon
Considered it to be a synonym of beauty
Truth is
It looks beautiful
Not because it glows beautifully
But
Just because it is a reflection of the light
Of the Sun
That gives it a glow
Just like

When someone tells me
That
When I read your poems
I feel love is flowing like a stream
and
How much of love you have

I can only smile

and say
It is not about how much I have loved

It is
But a reflection of love
That I have been blessed to have
That has inundated me so much
It reflects in the Sea of words
That you may call
Poetry